(3/09) ②

14 13 (12/09) ③ xcore

AnimalWays

Hawks

AnimalWays

Hawks

TOM WARHOL

Marshall Cavendish
Benchmark
New York

With thanks to Dr. Dan Wharton,
director of the Central Park Wildlife Center,
for his expert reading of this manuscript.

Marshall Cavendish Benchmark
99 White Plains Road
Tarrytown, NY 10591-9001
www.marshallcavendish.us

Library of Congress Cataloging-in-Publication Data
Warhol, Tom.
Hawks / Tom Warhol.
p. cm. — (Animalways)
Summary: Discusses the evolution, biology, life cycle, and social and mating behavior of
hawks and falcons.
Includes bibliographical references (p.   ) and index.
ISBN 0-7614-1744-3
1. Hawks—Juvenile literature. [1. Hawks. 2. Falcons.] I. Title. II. Series.
QL696.F32W355   2003   598.9'44—dc22   2003022138

Photo Research by Candlepants Incorporated

Cover Photo: Corbis/W. Perry Conway

The photographs in this book are used by permission and through the courtesy of: *Photo
Researchers*/Jim Zipp, title page, 69; Paul J. Fusco, 79; *Animals Animals*/Robert H. Armstrong,
9; Joe McDonald, 47; Ted Levin, 54; Zig Leszczynski, 60; JB Photographers, 63; Mark Jones,
82; Anthony Mercieca, 83; *Corbis*/Vanni Archive, 12 (left); Archivo Icono Grafico, 12 (right);
Canadian Museum of Civilization, 13; Francis G. Mayer, 15; Sygma/Pierre Vauthey, 17;
Hulton-Deutsch, 18; Galen Rowell, 19, 87, 93; Pangaea Designs, 24, 27; Jonathan Blair, 27;
Royalty Free, 29; Eric and David Hosking, 30 (left), 37; Joe McDonald, 30 (right), 78; Scott
T. Smith, 33; Nigel J. Dennis/Gallo Images, 35; Jamie Harron/Papillio, 39; William S. Clark/
Frank Lane Picture Agency, 43; Philip Perry/Frank Lane Picture Agency, 43; Peter Johnson,
51; Sygma/Caron (NPP) Philippe, 52; Ron Austing/Frank Lane Picture Agency, 57; Raymond
Gehman, 65; John Watkins/Frank Lane Picture Agency, 71; Wolfgang Kaehler, 73; Bryan
Knox; Papilio, 75; Fritz Polking/Frank Lane Picture Agency, 81; Lynda Richardson, 84; Adam
Woolfitt, 89; James L. Amos, 94; Layne Kennedy, 96; Kennan Ward, 97; *Minden Pictures*/
Tui de Roy, 100.

Printed in China

1 3 5 6 4 2

Contents

Animal Kingdom

CNIDARIANS

coral

ARTHROPODS
(animals with jointed limbs and external skeleton)

MOLLUSKS

squid

CRUSTACEANS

crab

ARACHNIDS

spider

INSECTS

grasshopper

MYRIAPODS

centipede

CARNIVORES

lion

SEA MAMMALS

whale

PRIMATES

orangutan

HERBIVORES
(5 orders)

elephant

ANNELIDS

earthworm

CHORDATES
(animals with
a dorsal
nerve chord)

ECHINODERMS

starfish

PHYLA

VERTEBRATES
(animals with a
backbone)

**SUB
PHYLA**

FISH

fish

BIRDS

HAWK

MAMMALS

AMPHIBIANS

frog

REPTILES

snake

CLASSES

RODENTS

squirrel

INSECTIVORES

mole

MARSUPIALS

koala

SMALL MAMMALS
(several orders)

bat

ORDERS

1 Hawks in Nature and Culture

Nestled on a narrow cliff ledge above the sparkling blue Mediterranean Sea, the young falcon nestling, in its tiny view of the world, sees its mother hurtling toward it with a songbird in her talons. The chick can see many other falcons flying in the distance, but it knows that this one is its mother. A sudden gust throws the mother falcon slightly off course, but the cries and lunges of neighboring birds in the colony as well as her natural sense of navigation force her to quickly find her own nest again among the fifty others scattered across this cliff face. At last she lands on the crowded ledge with the day's meal. The chick, along with its four siblings, screeches and cries, eager for the fresh food. The mother begins tearing the dead bird apart with her beak, passing small, bite-size pieces to her young.

All around them on other ledges in this broad, inaccessible cliff face above the crashing surf, other mothers are feeding other young. The songbird migration is good this year, providing

NORTHERN HARRIERS HUNT RODENTS AND OTHER SMALL PREY IN MARSHY AREAS LIKE THIS ONE IN JUNEAU, ALASKA.

the falcons with plenty of food; they timed their breeding period just right. These young chicks will grow quickly and will soon be able to join their parents in the daily hunt, taking their place in a wall of falcons that will intercept some of the great number of songbirds passing through this migration corridor.

Hawks: Vital Predators

These birds, known as Eleonora's falcons, are unusual among hawks and falcons in that they nest in colonies. Although many of these birds are solitary hunters, soaring the skies alone in search of their prey, they can also be social animals. But most species only socialize at certain times of the year, usually during breeding and migration.

Hawks and falcons are raptors, or birds of prey, meaning they catch and eat live creatures. The raptor group also includes the other large predatory, or hunting, birds of the world: eagles, kites, vultures, and owls. Many people use the term "hawk" to refer to other birds in the raptor group as well. For the purposes of this book, "hawk" will be used to mean all the diurnal, or daytime-active, raptors except for eagles and vultures; this includes true hawks, accipiters, harriers, kites, and falcons. Owls are nocturnal, or nighttime-active, raptors that are not directly related to the other raptor groups.

While catching and eating live prey can be a difficult task, especially for such a relatively lightweight creature, raptors have evolved to be one of the most successful groups of animals on the planet. They have keen eyesight, strong legs, sharp talons, and they are powerful fliers.

Hawks and falcons come in many shapes and sizes, from the 1.6-ounce (45-gram) Bornean falconet to the 9-pound (4-kilogram) crested caracara. Their differences have evolved as these birds have adapted to their surroundings and their chosen prey. The tiny falconet feeds mostly on insects, while the caracara feeds on small mammals and carrion. A group of hawks known as the accipiters specializes in hunting birds; they have long legs and are very quick and agile fliers, able to chase down a song-bird and snatch it out of the air. The snail kite has an especially long, thin beak that serves as the perfect tool for prying open the shells of its main prey, snails. The northern harrier's especially long legs are helpful for seizing small rodents out of the grass as it cruises low over grasslands and dunes.

Such amazing adaptations and hawks' remarkable hunting ability are attributes that have earned the respect, fear, and anger of mankind. For as long as humans have been around, hawks have played a role in their lives, whether as objects of inspiration or persecution.

Hawks in Culture

In many ancient cultures, hawks and other raptors were wor-shipped as companions, messengers to the gods, and in some cases, even as gods themselves.

Egyptians worshipped Horus, a falcon god whose image may have been inspired by the Lanner falcon. The eye of Horus was a popular amulet to wear and was said to promote good health. Falcons were also buried in tombs of important persons to accompany them to the next world. The griffin, a protective creature with the body of a lion and the wings and head of a raptor, was another figure in Egyptian mythology, and it also played an important role in many other cultures for centuries.

The huge numbers of raptors that migrate across the Sinai Peninsula and the many resident species in the Middle East inspired both respect and fear in the peoples of Israel. There are many references to birds of prey in the Bible. For example, the book of Leviticus states that eating blood is a sin, so Jews considered raptors unclean and would not eat them. They also feared being eaten by raptors and considered it a curse. Consequently, the Jewish culture is one of the only ones in the Middle East in which the practice of falconry, the art of hunting with birds, plays no part.

Hawks are strong and respected figures in cultures in the Americas. One of the three major figures in Inca culture in South America was a raptorlike human, with wings and a hooked beak, called the Thunderer. All hawks—or *waman* in Quechua, their native language—were very well respected. The Incas

FALCONS FIGURED PROMINENTLY IN EGYPTIAN MYTHOLOGY. THIS STATUE IS OF HORUS, THE FALCON GOD.

THE GRIFFIN SYMBOLIZES GREAT STRENGTH, EARNING IT A PLACE IN ARTWORK AND MYTH. MANY COUNTRIES HAVE ADOPTED IT AS THEIR SYMBOL.

recognized their talents as smart, swift, and brave hunters. The sharp-shinned hawk, *k'illi*, the caracara, *quoriquenque*, and the eagle, *anka*, were held in especially high regard. The stark black-and-white plumage of the caracara was used in the clothing and decorations of the Inca rulers.

In the Amazon basin, the Shavanté people used the primary flight feathers of the Cooper's hawk on their arrows because they knew this bird to be a fast flier and expert hunter. The Amahuaca of Peru took on the power of the hawk by smearing the juice from boiled hawk talons on their bodies before they hunted. Some North American Indians also revere raptors; the most important one is the golden eagle. Raptor feathers are often used in headdresses to show social status. In modern Mexico, people hang the feet of hawks and owls in trucks and buses as protection, to ward off evil and bad luck.

EAGLES AND HAWKS WERE IMPORTANT FIGURES TO THE TSIMSHIAN NATIVE AMERICAN TRIBE OF NORTHWEST NORTH AMERICA. THE TOTEM POLES THEY CARVED OFTEN FEATURED A RAPTOR HEAD.

Some peoples in northern Borneo in Malaysia pray to hawks as gods before working in their fields or going to war. They place wooden statues of birds of prey in front of houses to ward off evil spirits.

The Australian Aboriginal people also respected raptors. Each person had a totem or protective figure in the form of an animal. But these people did not worship them or other animals as gods. Sometimes they even hunted raptors for food and to use the birds' feathers for decoration. The Aborigines' stories helped to instruct their people about how to behave and also provide important practical information like hunting techniques.

For example, one Aboriginal story tells of two brothers, Eagle and Falcon, who hunt kangaroos together. Tracking some kangaroos to a cave, Eagle goes in to scare them out, while Falcon waits at the entrance to catch them. But Eagle becomes selfish and sends the thin ones out, keeping the fat ones for himself. This angers Falcon, who sets a fire at the mouth of the cave, so that when Eagle runs out he scorches his feathers. This teaches Eagle a lesson about being selfish. The Aborigines say that this is why the wedge-tailed eagle, common in Australia, has black feathers and why falcons often pester eagles, chasing them out of their territories.

You can see respect for hawks in the artwork of the Chinese during the Sung Dynasty (960 to 1279 C.E.). They were great bird artists who were especially fond of birds of prey. They often made very detailed and accurate drawings from memory. The art reflects the Chinese culture's great respect for these creatures as fellow inhabitants of the world, not figures to be worshipped or feared, as in many other cultures.

Western bird artists didn't produce any bird art at a comparable level of artistry until the 1800s. John James Audubon of the United States was the best known of these artists. Between

1827 and 1838 he produced his greatest book, *The Birds of America*, which includes more than 1,065 figures. He drew birds life-size from freshly killed specimens.

Falconry

Although in more recent history raptors have been hunted by humans, there was a time when humans actually hunted with hawks. Since at least 705 B.C.E.—the date of the earliest known record of falconry from Assyria—men used hawks to hunt small game, like rabbits. Watching wild hawks hunt, people realized how skilled these creatures were at catching their prey. It wasn't long before they captured some hawks, got them comfortable "on the glove," and taught them to hunt and return with their kill.

Falconry became very popular in the East—in China during the Han Dynasty (206 to 220 C.E.) and in India during the fourteenth century. It also became a popular sport in the Middle and Near East, where it remains so today. Persia (modern-day Iran) was the center of falconry in this region. Although falconry had long been practiced principally for subsistence, or a means of obtaining food, today many people in the region hunt for sport; it has become more of a social event, bringing families together for seasonal outings. But the Arab peoples' love for the sport and for the birds remains strong. The president of the United Arab Emirates (UAE), His Highness Sheikh Zayed bin Sultan Al Nahyan, has used some of his country's wealth to advance raptor conservation. He has helped to restore endangered wildlife prey species for raptors, and he has built a state-of-the-art veterinary hospital and research facility for birds of prey.

Falconry was introduced to Europe in the sixth century. It first came to Italy and then quickly spread to other countries. It was a popular sport there for more than a thousand years, and not just for the nobility. People of all social classes, even women and nuns, practiced falconry and kept falcons and hawks. The birds were very highly valued and were well cared for. An elaborate culture grew up around the sport, with special language and tools, like leather hoods to calm the birds when not hunting, gloves to protect the falconer's hand, and jesses, or tethers, to hold on to the bird's feet.

The sport's popularity waned in the eighteenth and nineteenth centuries as agriculture became more important, the social structure of royalty—the nobility were major practitioners and supporters of falconry—broke down, and guns were invented, making hunting with raptors less practical.

As its name suggests, falcons are the most popular species used in falconry. (Technically, a person who hunts with an eagle or

THE LEATHER HOOD OVER THE HEAD OF THIS HUNTING FALCON IN DUBAI (ONE OF
THE UNITED ARAB EMIRATES) KEEPS THE BIRD CALM BEFORE AND AFTER THE HUNT.

At the height of falconry's popularity in Europe, noblewomen kept small birds, like peregrine falcons.

a hawk is an austringer, but "falconry" is commonly used to mean all hunting with birds.) The preferred bird was the female peregrine falcon because it is not too large but is still capable of handling a wide variety of game, both in size and type. Since this

HARRIS'S HAWKS ARE THE PREFERRED SPECIES TODAY FOR HUNTING AND EDUCATIONAL PURPOSES BECAUSE THEY ARE MORE EASILY TRAINED THAN OTHER SPECIES.

species became endangered in the United States during the 1970s, people now practice the sport mostly with the Harris's hawk.

As recently as 1982, there were an estimated 10,000 to 20,000 falconers in the world, mostly in the Middle East, Europe, and North America. The regulations governing the sport today are very strict. Tests must be taken, licenses must be obtained, and only captive-bred birds may be used so the wild populations are not harmed in any way.

2 Origins

Though falconry has been practiced for a long time—more than 2,700 years—the period of man's association with raptors is a mere blip alongside these marvelous creatures' own history. Birds have evolved over millions of years, and because of their long history and their adaptability, they have become the most successful land animals on the planet. They live in almost every ecosystem on every continent. Today there are more than 9,000 species of birds, compared with about 3,000 species of amphibians, 6,000 species of reptiles, and 4,000 species of mammals. Some estimates of the total number of birds in the world are as high as 300 billion.

Where did they come from? How did these creatures evolve? They look almost nothing like any other animal species—unless you look very closely, that is. For centuries, evolutionary scientists have suspected a link between birds and reptiles. This suspicion began to gain some credibility with the finding in

ALTHOUGH PROBABLY NOT A GREAT FLIER, *ARCHAEOPTERYX* WAS ONE OF THE FIRST ALMOST FULLY FEATHERED ANCESTORS OF MODERN BIRDS. NOTE THE REPTILIAN FACE AND TEETH.

Germany in the 1860s of the first fossil showing both bird and reptile characteristics. This species was named *Archaeopteryx*, which means "ancient wing," and was thought to have lived during the Jurassic period about 150 million years ago. For more than a century this was the only known fossil to connect birds with reptiles, and scientists praised it as the missing link.

But many details about *Archaeopteryx* bothered other scientists. Why would there be only one species? How did this one evolve? What were its immediate ancestors and descendants? Eventually other specimens were unearthed and in the 1990s our knowledge of the evolution of birds grew enormously as many more new fossils were found. All of these, such as *Confusciornis* from China, were roughly the same age or younger than *Archaeopteryx*. As a result, it was thought that *Archaeopteryx* was the first creature to develop feathers. This and other theories of bird evolution will probably change and develop as more fossils are found.

In fact, in 1983 a fossil specimen of a birdlike creature was found that is thought to be about 75 million years older than *Archaeopteryx*, meaning that it evolved along with the earliest dinosaurs. Some scientists now suggest that *Archaeopteryx* was a "living fossil" in the Jurassic period, and that the species originally evolved much earlier, perhaps at the end of the Triassic period about 210 million years ago. These findings are still controversial and have yet to be completely accepted by the scientific community.

Ancient Predators

Picture all the land in the world clumped together along the Equator and drifting northward in a vast ocean. North America is joined with Europe, and South America with Africa; Antarctica and Australia fit in along the bottom. This is what the world looked like during the Triassic period, from 245 to 208 million years ago. If you look at a map of the world now, you can actually see how the continents once fit together: the swelling of western Africa fits nicely against the east coast of North America, and South America would tuck in below them.

This is also the world into which the dinosaurs evolved. The climate was warm and tropical, the land was not as uneven and mountainous as it is now, and life flourished. Many of these dinosaurs were four-legged herbivores. A group of carnivorous dinosaurs called theropods walked on their two rear legs and they used their front legs to catch and hold prey. Some of these ancient reptiles also had evolved primitive feathers on their tails and front legs, probably for warmth, camouflage, display, or other purposes.

One group of these creatures, called the dromaeosaurs (like the velociraptors in the movie *Jurassic Park*), ran around this ancient world in packs, catching insects and small mammals, even climbing trees to get to their prey. Some may have begun jumping from one tree to the next while chasing large insects, such as dragonflies. As these jumping dromaeosaurs became more successful, their primitive feathers became more specialized— longer, stiffer, and more aerodynamic—to help them glide between the trees and to slow their descent to the ground. These creatures became the ancestors of modern birds.

As the continents began breaking up near the end of the Triassic period, a mass extinction occurred, probably caused by meteors crashing into Earth, spewing up ash and debris that blocked the sunlight and changed the climate of the planet. Dinosaurs were among the animals that survived, and because many other animals died, the world became more hospitable to these dinosaurs. Many evolved into larger sizes and became dominant during the Jurassic (208 to 144 million years ago) and

VELOCIRAPTORS WERE RELATIVES OF EARLY BIRDS. THE FEATHERS ON ITS HEAD AND CHEST MIGHT HAVE BEEN FOR WARMTH OR DISPLAY PURPOSES.

Cretaceous (144 to 65 million years ago) periods. Other smaller dinosaurs—like the dromaeosaurs, who were evolving into birds—also survived and expanded their range and numbers. Many bird species, like *Archaeopteryx*, evolved during these

GEOLOGICAL TIMELINE

Era	Period	Epoch	Years Ago	Event
CENOZOIC	QUATERNARY	HOLOCENE	present 20,000-50,000	All modern bird forms evolved; Mass extinction—teratorns, mammoths, and bison
		PLEISTOCENE	100,000	All modern bird genera established
	TERTIARY	PLIOCENE	2 million	Beginning of Ice Ages
		MIOCENE	5 million	Teratorns alive; first Falconidae fossils
		OLIGOCENE	24 million	First Accipitridae and osprey fossils
		EOCENE	37 million	First appearance of raptorlike birds
		PALEOCENE	58 million	Bird and mammal diversity expands; Continents formed, moving to current positions
			65 million	
MESOZOIC	CRETACEOUS		66 million	Mass extinction, killing dinosaurs and leaving many birds alive; Waterbirds and toothed birds evolve; Flowering plants appear; Birds evolve worldwide
			144 million	*Confusciusornis* alive
	JURASSIC		150 million	*Archaeopteryx* alive; Pangaea begins to separate into Laurasia and Gondwana
			208 million	
	TRIASSIC		210 million	Mass extinction; First mammals; Breakup of Pangaea into Laurasia and Gondwana
			225 million	Theropods and thecodonts begin to evolve; First dinosaurs
			245 million	
PALEOZOIC	PERMIAN			Pangaea, a single supercontinent, forms; Mass extinction—most marine life and some mammal-like reptiles died out
	PENNSYLVANIAN		286 million	First reptiles
	MISSISSIPPIAN		320 million	
	DEVONIAN		360 million	Mass extinction
	SILURIAN		408 million	First land plants
	ORDOVICIAN		438 million	Mass extinction
	CAMBRIAN		505 million	
			570 million	
PRECAMBRIAN TIME			4.6 billion	Earliest fossil of life form

time periods as well. Birds filled a completely different ecological niche, or place in an ecosystem, than the dinosaurs, staying small and light because they needed to fly.

Room to Move

Another mass extinction, at the end of the Cretaceous period, also probably triggered by the impacts of enormous meteors, spelled doom for many creatures during the next million years. The large dinosaurs, as well as some birds, many plants, and some ocean life, vanished. As horrible as these mass deaths were, this began what some scientists call "the age of mammals and birds." All the smaller life forms left alive could now expand and populate areas formerly occupied by the large dinosaurs. The continents had taken on their current forms and were continuing to separate, isolating some species from others.

By this time, birds had evolved to have the basic body structure seen today. Now they really began to move all over the world and evolve into specialized shapes and sizes to fit their new environments. Around 58 million years ago, during the Eocene epoch of the Tertiary period, the first raptors evolved. These were much larger than today's raptors, and many were scavengers, like *Neocathartes*, a vulturelike bird that picked up dead animals along lake shores. The largest flying bird, a teratorn called *Argentavis*, lived about 10 million years ago in the Miocene epoch. It was over 6 feet tall (2 m) with a wingspan of about 25 feet (8 m). Many more raptors began to evolve during the Tertiary period until, by the beginning of the Pleistocene epoch 2 million years ago, all the modern families and genera we know today were alive and established.

But many species alive then no longer exist because of another mass extinction that occurred about 10,000 years ago,

DESPITE ITS HUGE SIZE AND FEARSOME PRESENCE, THE PTEROSAUR, ONE OF THE FIRST
VERTEBRATES TO EVOLVE WINGS AND TAKE FLIGHT, PROBABLY ATE FISH AND INSECTS.

at the end of the Pleistocene epoch. At that time, many large
land mammals as well as the teratorns and seven species of
eagles became extinct. By about 20,000 to 50,000 years ago, the
bird species that we know today were alive, including hawks.

3 The World of Hawks

The defining characteristic of hawks, falcons, and other raptors is that they capture and eat live prey or feed on carrion. While other birds, such as robins, sometimes also eat live prey as part of a broad diet that includes fruits and seeds, raptors are adapted to hunt and kill. They rely on meat as their food source.

The word "raptor" comes from the Latin for "plunderer," one who steals, or robs by force. Some hawks, such as the caracaras, do steal prey from other animals—even other raptors—but that behavior is more common among eagles. For example, the bald eagle of North America commonly steals food (also known as pirating) from another raptor that fits into our group of hawks—the osprey.

OSPREY, HAWKS THAT SPECIALIZE IN CATCHING FISH, PREFER TO HUNT AND NEST NEAR CALM WATERS, SUCH AS FRESHWATER LAKES, SALTWATER BAYS, AND LAGOONS.

Classification

To understand all the many different species of hawks and falcons, these birds, as well as all other living organisms—plants, animals, fungi, and bacteria—a system of classification was developed that groups all living things based on their morphology. The different levels of this classification system start with the most general grouping and proceed to the most specific: domain, kingdom, phylum, class, order, family, genus, and species. New research with DNA is helping to define more closely the relationships between all the different species of birds.

WHILE PEREGRINE FALCONS (LEFT) AND RED-TAILED HAWKS (RIGHT) ARE MEMBERS OF THE SAME ORDER THAT INCLUDES ALL RAPTORS, FALCONIFORMES, THEY REPRESENT DIFFERENT FAMILIES—FALCONIDAE AND ACCIPITRIDAE, RESPECTIVELY.

All 312 diurnal raptors can be grouped into four families. Two of these families, Cathartidae and Sagittariidae, include the seven species of New World vultures and the secretary bird, respectively. The secretary bird is long-legged and mostly flightless, like an ostrich, but it is related to eagles. Continuing DNA analysis has led to considerable debate about the classification of vultures. Some results suggest that these birds are more closely related to storks, but others keep them grouped with the raptors. It may be a few more years before a final classification is developed.

All 221 birds in 46 genera in the remaining two families, Accipitridae and Falconidae, are the subject of this book. This example of the classification of the red-tailed hawk (from North and Central America) and the peregrine falcon (worldwide) shows how the system works for these two families:

	Red-tailed hawk	Peregrine falcon
Domain	Eucarya	Eucarya
Kingdom	Animalia	Animalia
Phylum	Chordata	Chordata
Class	Aves	Aves
Order	Falconiformes	Falconiformes
Family	Accipitridae	Falconidae
Genus	*Buteo*	*Falco*
Species	*jamaicensis*	*peregrinus*

The names by which these species are scientifically known are *Buteo jamaicensis* and *Falco peregrinus*, respectively. (In this binomial system, the genus name is always capitalized and the species name always begins with a lower-case letter; the whole name is italicized.) These Latin names are the best way for scientists to refer to these species because the same bird may be known by different common names in different parts of its range. For example, until fairly recently the peregrine falcon was called the "duck hawk" in North America because of its preference for eating waterfowl. These names also help show which hawks are more closely related. For example, we can tell that the red-tailed hawk (*Buteo jamaicensis*) and the Galápagos hawk (*Buteo galapagoensis*) are closely related because they share the same genus name, *Buteo*, even though they live in very different and distant parts of the world.

Species Accounts

While there is not enough room here to describe all the different kites, hawks, buzzards, bazas, cuckoo hawks, harriers, goshawks, sparrowhawks, caracaras, falcons, falconets, kestrels, and hobbies in these two families, this list presents a representative sample.

Hawks (*Accipitridae*)

This is the largest group of raptors and one of the largest bird families, as well the most diverse. They are found on all continents except Antarctica. Included in this group are the hawks, accipiters, buzzards, eagles, kites, Old World vultures, harriers, sparrowhawks, and goshawks. They come in many sizes, shapes, and flying abilities, and they prefer different prey. They kill mostly with their feet and carry prey in both feet. They build their nests of sticks in trees, on cliffs, or on buildings, and they squirt their droppings out and away from the nest. Most species in this group have a bony ridge above the eyes that may help to shade them from bright sun and shield them from damage as they crash through brush while chasing prey.

True hawks. Most birds in this group are larger and heavier than birds in other groups. They have long, broad wings and short, broad tails. They breed and hunt in varied habitats from open country to forested areas. There are fifty-two species in ten genera, and they occur all over the world, from the tropics to the arctic.

The **rough-legged hawk** (*Buteo lagopus*), or rough-legged buzzard as this bird is known in Europe, breeds in the arctic and subarctic regions of the world, amid tundra and along mountainsides from northern Canada to Scandinavia and northern Eurasia. These large, bulky hawks cruise low over the open country,

ROUGH-LEGGED HAWKS PREFER TO HUNT OPEN COUNTRY LIKE GRASSLANDS AND FARMLANDS, SO THEY CAN OFTEN BE SEEN PERCHING ON UTILITY WIRES AND POLES.

taking advantage of seasonal population increases of voles and lemmings. Sometimes they will hunt by hovering over the tundra or open fields, unusual behavior for a hawk. Once winter arrives and their prey goes into hibernation, the hawks' migration route takes them south into the prairies, farmlands, marshes, and dunes of the United States, central and eastern Europe, and central Asia.

The rough-legged hawk has a rounded head, prominent brow, small bill, and long wings and tail. This is one of the few hawk species to have feathers all the way down their short legs to the toes. Their plumage varies among individuals, but generally they are mostly dark brown with pale markings above—on their backs and upperwing coverts (the feathers on top of their wings)—and with white or cream-colored breast and underwing coverts (feathers on the underside of their wings) and brown chest band below. In North America another color variation, or morph, is dark above and below.

Harriers and harrier-hawks. These slender hawks have long, narrow wings and long tails. They hunt open areas like grasslands, dunes, and heath glades by gliding low and slowly over the ground, looking for small rodents to pluck out of the vegetation with their long legs. Their facial ruff, a disk of feathers circling the face, helps them to locate prey in the dense grass by focusing sound toward their large ears, much like an owl. There are fifteen species in two genera. The two species of harrier-hawks, also known as gymnogenes in Europe and Africa, have double-jointed knees that allow them to reach into tree cavities and holes in the ground to pull out small birds or rodents.

African marsh harriers (*Circus ranivorus*) live year-round near large water bodies in the tropical regions of eastern and southern Africa. These birds may move around in search of food when water levels drop too low. As they glide slowly, about 16

DAMMING AND DRAINAGE OF THE WETLAND HABITATS OF THE AFRICAN MARSH HARRIER HAVE CAUSED THE NUMBERS OF THIS PREDATOR TO DECLINE SIGNIFICANTLY.

to 65 feet (5 to 20 m) above ground, their facial ruff, edged with white feathers, helps them to hear small mammals among the reeds at the water's edge. Or they may "harry" a waterfowl, hovering above the water, forcing the duck to dive and surface many times until it is exhausted and can be easily picked off.

Osprey. This bird is usually grouped with hawks but is really the only one of its kind. It has its own subfamily, Pandioninae.

The **osprey** (*Pandion haliaetus*) is similar to the accipiters, but different in that it specializes in catching fish. So it lives and breeds near clear and calm open water, both freshwater and coastal, in a wide range from Europe, Asia, and Africa to North and South America. Its strong feet, scaled for protection, have special pointed scales, called spicules, on the bottoms that help it grab slippery fish.

The osprey will often dive feet-first into the water, sometimes completely submerging before rising up carrying a fish in its long, curved talons. Its outer toes can then slide around to the back of the foot (no other diurnal raptor can do this) to make it easier to grab the fish and carry it away. Another adaptation to hunting fish is the osprey's oily plumage, which repels water.

Although it is the size of many hawks, the osprey's habitat, appearance, behavior, and prey make it easy to identify in the wild. It is a special treat to see this dark brown bird with white undersides, dark wrist patches, and bright white head with a dark mask hovering over a bay or lake as it scans for fish.

Accipiters and allies (sparrowhawks and goshawks). There are fifty-five species in six genera in this group. *Accipiter*, with forty-seven species, is the largest of any raptor genus. Closely related to the true hawks, these fast and agile hunters are smaller and have short, rounded wings and long tails—perfect for chasing birds in dense forests and scrublands. Of all raptors they show the greatest size difference between males and females.

Most of the world's population of the **northern goshawk** (*Accipiter gentilis*), the largest of the accipiters, live year-round as far north as the tree limit, from Canada across the globe through Europe and Siberia to the Pacific Ocean. Some of the more northerly populations move south for the winter, and those in mountainous areas move to lower elevations. These agile birds like tall coniferous, or evergreen, forests near openings and streams, where they have room to maneuver as they hunt grouse, thrushes, crows, rabbits, and squirrels.

Some of these hawks have adapted to live in European city parks, hunting pigeons, crows, and starlings. These aggressive

NORTHERN GOSHAWKS OFTEN HUNT FROM A PERCH IN A TREE, DIVING DOWN ON THEIR PREY AND SOMETIMES ENGAGING IN HIGH-SPEED CHASES THROUGH THE FOREST.

accipiters will even hunt other raptors and owls, and they are very protective of their nest sites, swooping down on intruders.

The goshawk's striking plumage—black cap and mask with a dark back and white underparts with beautiful dark barring—along with its fierce orange-red eyes make it a fearsome predator. Its average wingspan is 42 inches (1.1 m) and average weight is 1.8 pounds (816 g) for males and 3.3 pounds (1.5 kg) for females.

The **tiny hawk** (*Accipiter superciliosus*), true to its name, is the smallest accipiter, about the size of a thrush (a robin or mockingbird, for example). An average male weighs only 2.4 ounces (69 g) and an average female, 4.4 ounces (125 g). Their average wingspan is 17 inches (43 cm). Not much is known about these small and secretive sparrowhawks. They are easy to miss and hard to study in their year-round territories in Central and South America. Quick and agile, they dart out from their low perches along forest edges and clearings to snatch hummingbirds from tree branches or even from the air. With bright red eyes, a dark back, and barred undersides, they are similar in appearance to the northern goshawk but without the black mask.

Kites. This may be the most primitive of all hawk groups, with less-evolved hunting skills than the accipiters and true hawks. With weaker bills and talons, they can't kill large animals and so feed mostly on insects, reptiles, amphibians, and snails. Kites also tend to be social, sometimes nesting in colonies where food is abundant. The nineteen species in ten genera are mostly found near water in the warmer regions of the world.

The brightly colored **Brahminy kite** (*Haliastur Indus*) can commonly be seen along coasts, waterways, and in rice paddies in India, Indonesia, and many other South Asian island nations. This bird's bright white head and breast atop its rich chestnut wings and body make it easy to identify as it soars over waters and marshy areas searching for fish, frogs, snakes, crabs, and insects. This kite also lives comfortably alongside humans and can be a common sight in harbors hunting fish, at garbage dumps feeding on refuse, and along roadsides eating carrion.

This close association with humans probably inspired the Brahminy kite's use as a figure in Eastern religion. The Brahminy kite is said to have served Vishnu, a powerful and protective god who is one of the three major deities in the Hindu religion.

THE BROWNISH FEATHERS ON THIS IMMATURE BRAHMINY KITE'S HEAD WILL EVENTUALLY MOLT INTO THE ALL-WHITE FEATHERS THAT MAKE THIS SPECIES SO STRIKING.

Unfortunately, not all people respect this beautiful raptor. On the island nation of Java, the kite population is declining because of persecution, habitat loss, and poisoning.

Honey-buzzards, bazas, and cuckoo-hawks. These birds are unusual even for kites, of which they are a subgroup. They don't have the bony shield above their eyes like most hawks and some other kites. Instead, they have special feathers that help protect their eyes from their main prey—bees, wasps, and hornets. The fifteen species in seven genera all live in tropical areas.

The **western honey-buzzard**'s (*Pernis apivorus*) preference for searching out ground nests of bees, wasps, and hornets keeps it near the ground and makes it less easily seen than other large

THE FEATHERS ON THE FOREHEAD AND AROUND THE EYES OF HONEY-BUZZARDS ARE SMALLER AND GROW MORE DENSELY TO PROTECT THEM FROM THE STINGS OF THE BEES AND WASPS THAT ARE THEIR PREY.

raptors. Because of this and the bird's variable plumage, it is hard to find and identify. It breeds in open forests, glades, and heathlands in Europe and western Eurasia and spends the winter in open woodlands, along forest edges, and among the wooded savannas of southern Africa.

This clever hunter sits perched, watching for bees gathering nectar, then follows the bees back to their nests. When a honey-buzzard finds a ground nest, it will dig down up to one foot deep (30 cm) into the earth to get to it. It will eat the honeycombs, larvae, pupae, and adults. This honey-buzzard also hunts on the wing; it is quick enough to snatch flying ants and termites out of the air with its beak.

Falcons *(Falconidae)*

This is the most distinctive group of raptors and includes falcons, caracaras, and forest-falcons. These birds are found throughout the world; many species live in South America. They kill with both their beaks and their feet, carry their prey in one foot, and eat small stones to aid digestion. Some falcons have a tooth or notch on their upper mandible, or beak, which they use to snap the neck of their prey. Unlike hawks, falcons do not have a bony ridge over the eyes. They also do not build stick nests like most other raptors but scratch a shallow depression on cliff ledges or rooftops or use the nests of other birds, such as crows, woodpeckers, or other raptors. Instead of shooting their droppings out and away from their nests like hawks, falcons excrete directly over the side of their nests.

Caracaras and forest-falcons. These two kinds of falcons are found only in the warmer regions of the New World—North, Central, and South America. The unusual caracaras are mostly carrion feeders. They have more exposed skin around their ceres, or upper bill, than other hawks; this trait is shared by vultures, birds that also eat carrion. This helps to prevent blood and gore from sticking to feathers near the face and nostrils, where infectious bacteria could enter the body. The forest-falcons are very secretive, living in dense forest in the tropics and subtropics, so not much is known about them. These two groups have seventeen species in seven genera.

Crested caracaras *(Caracara plancus)*, or carancos, have a very widespread range, from the southern tip of South America to eastern Brazil, and from Central America through Mexico into Arizona, Texas, and Florida. While they aren't migratory in this range, they are nomadic, which means they wander around in search of food, not sticking to one territory. They can also take advantage of a wide variety of habitats, from open country to ranchland and coconut plantations, as well as mountainous areas, beaches, and marshes.

Crested caracaras are the largest of the nine species of caracaras. These chunky birds with large bills and bright pink ceres are not swift hunters like the accipiters. They feed mostly on carrion and slow-moving prey, such as turtles or young and injured mammals. They will often take advantage of stranded fish, roadkill, or even dead cattle. Killing young sheep often gets them shot by ranchers. The deforestation in Central and South America that is causing many other raptor populations to drop has actually benefited the crested caracara, since many of these cutover areas are used for cattle and sheep ranches.

The **barred forest-falcon** (*Micrastur ruficollis*) is another secretive Central and South American falcon. Although they are hard to find, scientists think the population of this species is greater than any other New World tropical raptor. They are mostly active at dawn and dusk in the dense tropical forests, hunting for geckos and other lizards, as well as small birds and insects. Perching low in the forest, they sometimes follow swarms of army ants, darting down with fast wing beats and agile turns while snatching up prey displaced by the ants. Like the harriers, they have a slight facial ruff and large ear holes that help them locate prey by sound—very unusual for a falcon.

True falcons and falconets. True falcons are among the most numerous of all raptor species. They are generally small, fast, agile flyers, hunting everything from insects to birds. Their streamlined shape and long, narrow wings and tails enable them to catch their prey in the air, twisting and turning perfectly through dense vegetation. The forty-six species in three genera live in all parts of the world.

The bold and handsome **red-headed falcon** (*Falco chicquera*), or turumti, can usually be found among open groves of palmyra or Borassus palms in India and southern Africa. It catches most of its prey—birds and occasionally bats—while flying low to the ground, or even sometimes swooping up suddenly toward a bird flying above it. These falcons don't migrate or travel very far, and pairs hunt together in a relatively small territory. They time their breeding to coincide with the songbird migration so the chicks will have plenty to eat.

THE RED-HEADED FALCON PREYS MAINLY ON SMALL BIRDS. AS A RESULT, IT HAS DEVELOPED SHORT, BLUNT WINGS THAT ENABLE IT TO MANEUVER QUICKLY IN FLIGHT.

IDENTIFYING HAWKS IN FLIGHT

One of the more challenging and exciting aspects of birding is trying to identify a hawk circling overhead or hunting in an open field. Identification can be much easier when you understand a few basic ideas about the shapes, habitats, and flight patterns of broad groups of hawks and falcons.

Accipiters *Size:* small to large
Shape: short, rounded wings, and long tail
Habitat: forested areas
Flight: gliding mixed with three or more rapid wing beats; "dash and grab" hunting

True hawks *Size:* medium to large
Shape: long, broad wings, and short, wide tails
Habitat: fields and forests; often seen on perches
Flight: soaring

Osprey *Size:* large
Shape: gull-like, narrow wings often bent at wrist
Habitat: water bodies, especially near coast
Flight: hovering, gliding

Harriers *Size:* medium to large
Shape: long, narrow wings, and long tail
Habitat: grasslands, dunes
Flight: slow gliding low to ground; wings in dihedral, or V

Kites *Size:* medium
Shape: short, stout, hooked bills; pointed wings (falconlike); tails short to long, forked in some species
Habitat: warm climates near water
Flight: kiting, or motionless gliding

Falcons *Size:* small to large
Shape: large, square heads; long, pointed wings; long tails
Habitat: fields, meadows, grasslands
Flight: very quick gliding, stooping (some kestrels hover)

They are somewhat similar in color and markings to the widespread peregrine falcon or the American kestrel. A rufous crown and nape sit above a slim black mask, white cheeks, and dark brown eyes. Their gray back and black primary feathers contrast with their white and variously barred undersides and yellow legs.

As its name suggests, the **Philippine falconet** (*Microhierax erythrogenys*) lives only on the Philippine Islands. Weighing less than 2 ounces (57 g), this tiny bird perches near streams or clearings. When it spots an insect, such as a dragonfly or moth, it dashes out to quickly snatch it up in its beak, then carries the prey back to the same perch to eat it. With its dark, glossy black back and cap, bright white undersides, and pointed wings, the Philippine falconet is similar to a swallow in appearance as well as behavior. Like the barred forest-falcon, this falconet nests in tree cavities, often old woodpecker nest sites.

4 Hawks Are Made of ...

The various hawk and falcon species seem very different in appearance and habits from each other. Each species is adapted to very specific habitats—harriers to areas with low, grassy vegetation; caracaras to open areas with many places to find dead animals; and osprey to open water, where they can fish. But since all these birds are raptors, they all share a very similar body structure.

Anatomy

Being in the kingdom Animalia ourselves, we humans are well aware of the basic make-up of most animals. We have one head, two eyes, one mouth, two ears, and four limbs—in our case, two arms and two legs; in most other animals, four legs. Hawks are, of course, animals also, but they are very different from mammals because they are in the class Aves, meaning they are birds.

THE BRIGHT PLUMAGE OF THIS AMERICAN KESTREL IDENTIFY IT AS A MALE. THE DARK STRIPES NEAR THE EYE ARE COMMON AMONG RELATED FALCON SPECIES AND MAY SERVE TO REDUCE GLARE WHEN HUNTING.

As a result, they share all the basic anatomical features common to all birds. Some of the more obvious features are two legs for walking and grasping perches or prey; two wings for flying; a tail to aid in flying and balancing on perches; and a bill for carrying things and picking up, cracking open, or tearing apart food. Each bird species' body structure is geared toward finding a certain kind of food in a certain kind of habitat, like hawks hunting live prey. These amazing adaptations make raptors very skilled hunters.

Skeleton. Hawks and falcons are built for flight, from the skeleton outward. Although the bones of hawks are very strong and help them bring killing blows to many creatures, their bones actually weigh surprisingly little. They make up only a small percentage of the birds' total weight. This is because many of the bones are hollow, with crisscrossing supports that provide rigidity without too much extra weight. This is the key to hawks' success as aerial predators: they are strong and light.

A hawk's skull is also very lightweight because of the sockets that house its very large eyes, important tools for a flying hunter. One of the largest bones in a hawk's body is the keel bone. It sits below the chest and anchors the large flight muscles. The keel bone and other bones attached to the flight muscles are protected from the bird's strong wing beats by another, more flexible bone called the furcula, or wishbone, which absorbs the stress of the beats.

The joints between the wing bones are also very important for flight. They are flexible to allow the bird to open and close its wings quickly, but the joints can also lock in place to provide the strength and firmness needed when the hawk is soaring in a strong wind.

Wings. While the light weight of a hawk's skeleton is one amazing adaptation to aid it in flight, the wings themselves are

Red-Tailed Hawk Head

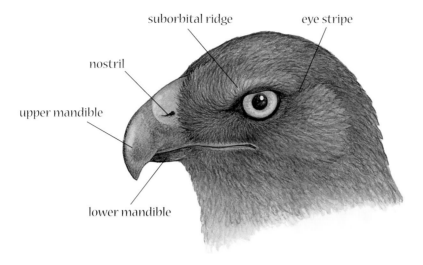

suborbital ridge

eye stripe

nostril

upper mandible

lower mandible

the most remarkable adaptation. Wings evolved from arms and hands, and much of the architecture remains remarkably similar. Many of the bones are the same, but most have been modified in one way or another. The wing can be divided into the arm, the wrist, and the hand.

The main flight feathers, or remiges, are the primaries, which are attached to the hand, and the secondaries, attached to the arm. The feathers on the top of the wing are called the upperwing coverts and the ones on the bottom are called the underwing coverts.

The outer primaries are notched or slotted. This allows the feathers to react to different wind conditions, stabilizing flight and increasing lift.

As with the rest of the body, the wings of a hawk or falcon are designed for different kinds of flight to suit their different prey:

- The true hawks have wide, rounded wings that help them to soar above fields while they search for rabbits, mice, or other prey.

Wings

upperwing

underwing

- Falcons have narrow, pointed wings that are perfect for high-speed chases—very useful when hunting birds in fields.

- Accipiters' wings are narrower than true hawks' but still rounded at the edges. This allows for quick flight but also good maneuverability as they chase birds through forested areas.

- Harriers have long, rounded wings that they hold in a V-shape, or dihedral angle, enabling them to hover low at slow speeds over grassy and marshy areas as they hunt for rodents.

- With their long, pointed wings, kites hold steady against the wind in an almost motionless glide called kiting, while they scan the ground and lake edge for insects, reptiles, or snails.

THE JACKAL BUZZARD IS AN EXAMPLE OF A TRUE HAWK, OR BUTEO. NOTE THE BROAD, ROUNDED WINGS WITH THE FEATHERS OF THE HAND SPREAD APART.

Beak and Talons. A raptor's beak and feet are its primary means of catching, killing, and eating food. Consequently, they need to be strong and sharp.

The beak and talons are made of bone covered with a tough material called keratin—like our fingernails and cows' hooves. This material constantly grows and is worn down with use. The beak is the heaviest part of a raptor's head. The upper mandible is long, curved, and hooked. The sides are thin and sharp, providing a knifelike edge to cut the meat against the sturdy lower jaw. Hawks use their beaks mostly for tearing apart

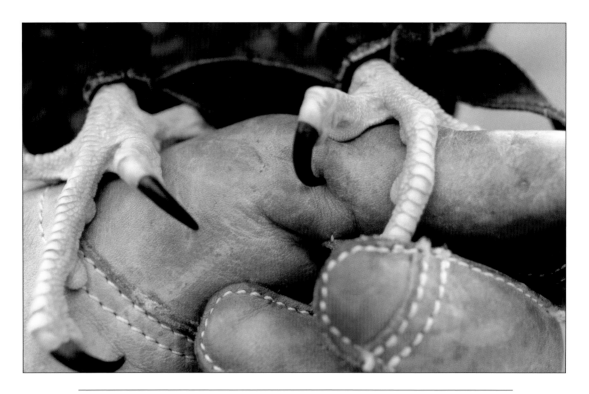

THE LONG TOES AND CURVED TALONS OF THIS RAPTOR ARE USEFUL FOR CATCHING QUICK PREY AND HOLDING IT FIRMLY WHILE THE BIRD EATS. FALCONERS PROTECT THEMSELVES FROM THE POWERFUL TALONS OF THEIR BIRDS WITH LEATHER GLOVES.

their prey once they've caught it with their feet. They don't use their beaks for killing; this avoids having their eyes or head injured by a fighting mammal. Falcons use both their feet and their beaks for killing. Some species have a special notch, or tooth, along the side of the upper mandible for grabbing and breaking the neck of their prey. Since they feed mostly on birds and insects, there is less chance of injury to their heads. Some beaks are especially adapted for eating certain foods. The snail kite's upper mandible is extra long and pointed for prying open snail shells and extracting the fleshy meat.

The cere, a usually brightly colored area of naked skin connected to the upper mandible, is easy to clean of blood and gore from the kill. This helps keep the birds free from any infection. The color of the cere often shows the age of the bird; it becomes more vibrant as the bird reaches sexual maturity and fades with increasing age.

The feet of hawks and falcons are very strong and adapted to their prey. Their tarsi, or legs below the knees, are covered in scales that help protect them from their prey. They have four toes, three facing forward and one facing backward. All of these end in talons. The inner and hind toes are the most powerful; they work together to crush the prey. The hind toe and talon are usually the longest and often deliver the killing blow.

The larger hawks that hunt larger animals have short, thick, strong tarsi and long, curved talons. These talons easily pierce the prey, puncturing vital organs; they also help to carry the kill away. Falcons and accipiters who hunt smaller, faster prey have longer, thinner tarsi and long, slender toes that give them a longer reach, so they can snatch up birds or small rodents as they try to flee.

Eyes. A hawk's eyes are the bird's most important tool. The vision of raptors is two to three times the strength of human vision. It allows them to see their prey from a great distance. Not only can they see farther, but they can see more detail. When a red-tailed hawk is soaring high above a field, he can see almost every creature that is moving through the dense grass.

One reason that hawks have such sharp eyesight is the size of their eyes. They are much larger relative to their body size than human eyes; more light enters larger eyes. They are also very long and deep, which gives hawks a great depth of vision. All this, combined with more sensitive cells in the retina and two foveae (pits in the back of the eye that help to focus vision; humans have just one), gives them very sharp and stereo-scopic vision.

Since hawks' eyes are encased in bone for protection, they cannot move very much. Instead, hawks turn their heads to look from side to side. The large size of hawks' eyes also makes them stick out farther from the eye socket than most animals' eyes. In some hawks and falcons, a bony brow extends out above the eye, both shading and protecting it. Also, a third, translucent (see-through) eyelid, called a nictitating membrane, closes protectively over the eye when the hawk pounces on prey or flies through dense vegetation.

The color of some hawks' eyes changes over the course of their lives. This helps us determine the age of a particular bird. For example, the variable goshawk is born with gray eyes, but these turn yellow by the end of its first year. Later, they turn orange, and when they are fully mature adults, their eyes become a deep red.

Metabolism

It takes a lot of work for a hawk or falcon to stay alive. Flying uses up a lot of energy—some types of flight use more energy than others. Also, raptors have to maintain a body temperature of about 101° F (38° C) to keep their lightweight bodies warm. Since meat is easier to digest than vegetable matter, birds of prey have a shorter and less muscular digestive system than herbivores. The food they eat passes through their bodies quickly.

When a hawk makes a small kill, it may eat the mouse, bird, lizard, or insect immediately. If the meal is too big to eat in one or two gulps, the hawk may pick it apart quickly. In either case, the food passes first into its crop. Later, when the bird is at rest in a safe place, the food passes slowly into the gizzard, which grinds the meat before passing it into the stomach.

Hawks swallow bones, fur, and feathers along with the meat, so the crop and gizzard are necessary to help break the food apart. But this leaves the birds with lots of waste in their systems. They deal with this by regurgitating pellets. These are small balls of the indigestible parts. Some bones of the smaller animals that hawks eat are still intact when they are regurgitated. Studying these pellets helps give scientists a good idea of a raptor's diet.

Plumage

Feathers are what defines a bird, and they also happen to be one of the most incredible adaptations that has ever evolved. There are three main types of feathers: contour flight, contour body, and downy feathers. All of these are made up of a rachis, or central shaft, to which are fused the barbs, or branches. The barbs are also branched into tiny hooks called barbules. One feather grasps on to the next using the barbules; this creates the continuous feather coat out of the individual feathers. If an individual feather becomes damaged, the bird can still fly, and a new feather will grow back in its place.

The symmetrical body feathers give a bird its general shape. The flight feathers, which make up the primary and secondary feathers of the wing, are asymmetrical. This is important for flight—the leading edge, the side facing into the wind, has shorter barbs than the trailing edge, reducing drag. The downy feathers, which lie next to the bird's skin, are not neat and evenly organized like the other feathers. They are shorter and more jumbled. Their tangled barbs help to provide insulation, keeping the bird warm while allowing air to flow. There are also other feathers that serve more specific functions, such as protecting the eyes and sensing the position of other feathers.

Hawk Feathers

contour flight

contour body

filoplume

bristle feather

semiplume

down feather

THE NORTHERN HARRIER IS ONE SPECIES OF HAWK THAT SHOWS A DRAMATIC
DIFFERENCE BETWEEN THE PLUMAGE OF MALE (RIGHT) AND FEMALE (LEFT) BIRDS.

Since there are so many species of hawks and falcons, it
follows that there is wide variety in their plumage. Although
there aren't too many different colors—mostly brown, red-brown,
black, gray, and white—there is a lot of variation in the combina-
tions and the way these colors are displayed on the coat.

Generally hawks are darker above, on the back and upper-
wings, and lighter below, on the chest, stomach, underwings,
and in some cases, legs. The upper parts tend to be either solid
or very faintly streaked or barred, while the undersides range
from very plain to boldly streaked or barred. The pattern on the

tail feathers is usually similar to that on the secondaries, while the pattern on the breast is often the same as that on the wing linings above the flight feathers.

These colors and patterns communicate information to others of their own species or even other species—a particular plumage will show the species, age, and physical condition of a bird. The coat can also be effective camouflage. Immature hawks and falcons are often patterned to blend with their environment to prevent the inexperienced bird from being attacked

Hawk Body

by a stronger predator. In some cases—the Cooper's hawk, peregrine falcon, and gray hawk, for example—immature birds are easy to distinguish because they have vertical streaking on their chests, while mature birds have horizontal streaking. It may take one or more years, depending upon the species, for juvenile hawks to mature and gain their adult plumage.

There are also differences in plumage between some male and female hawks of the same species. This difference is less obvious in hawks than it is in other birds, but the plumage of the adult males tends to be more colorful or vibrant than the duller, browner females. As in the juvenile birds, this is probably a camouflaging tool to protect females when they are nesting.

Size Differences

In most of the animal kingdom, size seems to matter. Most male mammals are larger than females of the same species. There are some obvious reasons for this: Males need to be larger to compete with other males for mates, their territories, and food. The larger and stronger a male is, the better chance he will have of reproducing and passing on the genes to his progeny, or young. This size difference is known by scientists as sexual dimorphism.

The reasons for size differences in hawk species are not as well understood. Hawks exhibit reverse sexual dimorphism—the females are larger than the males. The size differences vary from species to species, with bird-eaters like accipiters and falcons having the most differences (females may be twice the size of males) and scavengers like caracaras having the fewest differences. Since catching live birds is more difficult than feeding on carrion, some scientists think that the large differences in size between males and females of bird-catching raptors enables these hunters to take advantage of a wider variety of food.

THE VERTICAL BANDS ON THIS SHARP-SHINNED HAWK'S CHEST IDENTIFY IT AS AN
IMMATURE BIRD.

When songbirds are scarce or require too much energy to catch, the male may bring other prey, like insects or small mammals, back to the nest. And once the young are old enough for the female to leave the nest to help the male hunt, the parents can each hunt prey suited to its size; the female can focus on larger species and the male on smaller ones.

But there are many other theories to explain reverse sexual dimorphism. According to one, males evolved to be smaller because females tended to choose smaller males for mates as they were less of a threat to females and the young. Other scientists have suggested that maybe males are scarcer, so females need to compete for them: the larger the female, the better she is able to compete. Or females may be larger in order to better protect the young and keep them warm, since the female is the one who spends most of the time at the nest. Also, a larger female has more energy to produce a full clutch of eggs, which helps increase the species' survival.

5 Lifestyles of the Feathered and Taloned

The behavior of hawks is just as fascinating and varied as their physical makeup. Their choice of habitat, flying and hunting methods, prey, calls, and breeding habits all differ between the many species of hawks and falcons. However, the various species and groups of these masterful hunters share many common characteristics and traits. They are all looking for the same thing: to survive and reproduce. They do this by finding adequate food in areas with safe nest sites for raising their young.

Territories

Hawks and falcons make their homes in nearly all possible habitats on Earth, from tundra to desert and rain forest. Some species are capable of hunting and living in a variety of habitats.

AN AFRICAN PYGMY FALCON SITS ON ITS PERCH WITH ITS GECKO PREY
AFTER DIVING DOWN AND SNATCHING IT OFF THE GROUND.

These birds are called generalists, like the common kestrel, which breeds in areas from the cold tundra of Siberia to the hot, dry deserts of Africa. This falcon eats anything that it can catch, including voles, birds, reptiles, insects, and it even feeds on carrion.

Specialists have very particular habitat needs. This is usually because they hunt very specific prey. The snail kite's preference for apple snails restricts its habitats to freshwater wetlands in South America and the southern United States. The specialist species are often more vulnerable to becoming endangered or extinct. If snail populations suddenly crashed, many snail kites would die from starvation.

Hawks and falcons choose where they live based on two major factors: food and nest sites. Since food is not always available year-round in some places and nesting sites are limited in areas with year-round food, many species of raptor—and other birds—have two homes: a breeding territory and nonbreeding territory. This movement of animals from one home to another is known as migration.

The seasonal availability of food is dependent upon climate. Most of the land area in the world is concentrated in the northern hemisphere. In favorable climatic conditions, these large areas have plenty of food to support the large numbers of raptors. In temperate and boreal areas, such as North America, the cold, snowy winters slow or stop production of hawks' and falcons' food sources. Many prey creatures go into hibernation or are hidden beneath snow and ice. In response, many raptors and other birds move south into tropical and sub-tropical regions of Central and South America where there is a year-round supply of prey.

The reason that all raptors can't live and breed where there is food available all the time, such as in the tropics, is because there is less habitat in these areas. There are more mated pairs

THE SNAIL KITE IS SO SPECIFICALLY ADAPTED TO EATING SNAILS THAT THE SPECIES
MIGHT NOT SURVIVE IF SNAILS DISAPPEAR.

than there are suitable nest sites in the southern hemisphere.

Most hawks and falcons only maintain and defend a strict
territory during the breeding season. During the non-breeding
season, they may be more nomadic, moving around in search of
food. The different breeding ranges of raptors vary with their
size. The tiny pygmy falcons need less than 0.4 square mile (1
km^2), while the large martial eagle needs more than 116 square
miles (300 km^2) to meet its hunting needs. The prey's range

largely determines a hawk's range. A prey species with a large range means that the raptor that hunts it must have a large range. In most cases, a raptor aggressively defends its whole territory against other birds of the same species, but not necessarily against those of other species because other species of hawk or falcon are usually looking for different foods.

Most pairs nest alone in a large territory. A mating pair of hawks will reuse the same range from year to year unless habitat conditions change or a mate dies. These sites may be taken over by their young or others of the same species once the original pair dies, moves on, or is forced out of the territory. Some peregrine falcon cliff nests have been continuously occupied by this species for hundreds of years. Hanging on to a good nesting location helps the birds survive. If the site is safe and there is plenty of food around to feed their young, the birds use less energy to survive, keeping them strong and fit.

In some cases where food is plentiful, colonies may form, as in cliff-nesting Eleonora's falcons and sooty falcons, black-shouldered kites from Africa and India, and Australian letter-winged kites. Territories are still maintained around nest sites, but these are relatively small. For example, depending upon the nesting location, Eleonora's falcons may defend a territory from 6.5 feet (2 m) to 33 feet (10 m).

Migration

Having two homes means that most raptors move from one distinct range to another. These distances can be very great. Most of the population of Swainson's hawks migrates from Canada and the United States to South America. One banded bird's documented trip from Saskatchewan to Argentina was measured at 7,146 miles (11,500 km). The journey took four months to complete—that's 56 miles (90 km) a day. Some peregrine falcons travel about 9,300 miles (15,000 km), from Canada's Northwest Territories to Argentina.

Sometimes only part of a population, usually those birds on the northern and southern edges of the species' range, migrates. Only the northern goshawk individuals breeding in arctic Canada move south for the winter, passing over resident goshawks in central Canada and settling down in southern Canada and the northern United States.

There are more localized seasonal movements as well. Some hawks and falcons travel more locally within the species' range to where food is available. For example, in January many prairie falcons move into the open country of the western United States and breed in areas where their main prey, ground

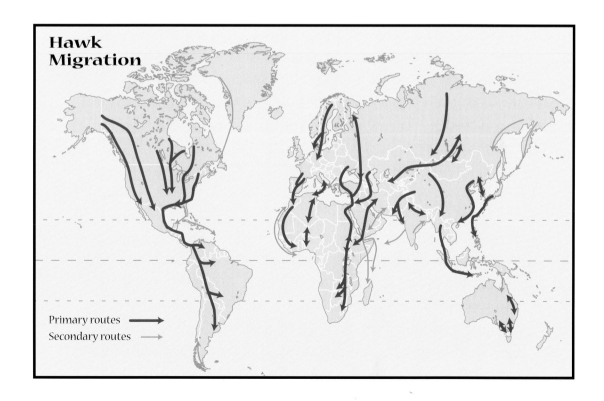

Hawk Migration

Primary routes →
Secondary routes →

squirrels, are emerging from estivation (similar to hibernation, but animals do it to escape drought instead of cold). In June, when the squirrels go back underground, the falcons disperse to find other, more widespread, prey.

Still other species are not faithful to specific breeding grounds because their food sources are less dependable. Australian letter-winged kites follow the populations of long-haired rats, which increase dramatically after heavy rains. The rains encourage growth of the plants that are the rats' food source. These kites may not breed at all during years-long dry spells. But when there is plentiful food, like the rats, the kites will have multiple broods in a season to make up for the dry years. When the rains end and the rats disappear, the kites disperse into new territories in search of other food.

Long-distance migratory hawks also have to deal with difficult travels and scarce food. These long trips take a lot out of the birds, and they are exhausted and much thinner when they arrive at their wintering grounds. Fortunately, some birds can find food along the way. Others, like Swainson's hawks, eastern red-footed falcons, and western honey-buzzards must put on extra weight before they head out on their long trip because food sources aren't reliable on their routes.

Carried by Winds

To help expend less energy on their long journeys, most migrating birds take advantage of air currents to keep them aloft. They follow two main types of air currents, called thermals and updrafts. But since these air currents don't occur uniformly across the landscape or over water at all, the birds have to pick their routes carefully. Thermals form as the sun heats open areas of the landscape, creating rising columns of air. Since the land is

THE FEATHERS ON THIS SWAINSON'S HAWK'S HAND, THE END OF ITS WING, ARE SPREAD APART TO HELP REDUCE AIR TURBULENCE AS THE HAWK SOARS.

uneven, these thermals occur patchily. Migrating raptors glide from one thermal to the next. As they reach a thermal, they allow the warm, rising air to lift them high up in the column. Once they reach the top, they drop and glide into the next thermal. Updrafts occur as wind masses hit mountain ranges, forcing the air up and over the top. That's why raptors can often be seen cruising above these ranges.

Since there are relatively few good migration routes that have reliable thermals and mountain updrafts, many species become concentrated at narrowed points on the landscape, such as peninsulas, mountain ridges, or coastlines, where currents become concentrated. Some of the narrower spots, as in Panama and Eilat, Israel, have become very popular spots for people to watch the millions of migrating raptors that pass overhead in the spring and fall. Numbers in the fall are greater because of the new population of juvenile birds, raised in the breeding season. Many juvenile birds die before it is time to head north again in the spring.

Hunting

Of all the ways to find food, hunting live prey is the most difficult and dangerous. When your food source is quick, has its own hiding places, can defend itself, and is being hunted by other creatures as well, you have to be very good at finding and killing it without getting yourself hurt or killed. Hawks and falcons hunt nearly every kind of living thing. Small raptors such as falcons tend to hunt insects, reptiles, small mammals, and small birds; accipiters hunt all sizes of birds, from songbirds to waterfowl; osprey hunt large fish; harriers hunt small mammals up to the size of ground squirrels; kites feed on insects, snails, reptiles, small rodents, and birds; and true hawks hunt a range of prey, from lizards to pheasants and prairie dogs.

Most birds of prey do their hunting alone, but even these solitary hunters sometimes hunt in pairs and share their kill. One bird chases or scares the prey while the other swoops in to grab the animal as it is trying to escape from the first. Harris's hawks, from the southwestern United States and Central and South America, are very social birds, both in their hunting and breeding habits. Two or three hawks may work cooperatively to chase and tire their prey. Or they may flush a rabbit out of its hole and into the waiting talons of another Harris's hawk at the rear entrance of the burrow. For this species, which hunts scattered prey over a wide-open landscape, cooperative hunting is more efficient than working alone.

Birds of prey use three main hunting methods. Although some species may be specialists, most use all of these methods at one time or another.

From the air. Many hawks and falcons, including osprey, harriers, kites, accipiters, and some falcons hunt from the air. Some birds will soar high above the ground, which helps them to scan a large area. But many prey animals have good eyesight and can see raptors soaring above them. So some raptors, like the harriers, fly low over the ground, using vegetation and other obstacles to hide them until they are almost on top of their prey. The peregrine falcon, which commonly hunts ducks, will dive at great speed with wings tucked close to its body. It will strike hard and rake its longer rear talon across the duck's back. This dive is called a stoop. The falcon will follow the duck as it falls to the ground.

THIS PEREGRINE FALCON MAY BE
ABLE TO CARRY AWAY THIS DUCK
THAT IT HAS ATTACKED. IF THE
DUCK IS TOO HEAVY, THOUGH, THE
FALCON WILL JUST HOLD ON TO IT
AS IT FLIES, GUIDING IT TO A SAFE
LOCATION TO EAT.

The American kestrel, a falcon, often hovers while it hunts, like an osprey, searching for voles, shrews, or insects in fields. But just as often, kestrels and other falcons are capable of chasing down very fast, flying prey and snatching it out of the air.

From perches. Accipiters, true hawks, and falcons also commonly hunt from perches. Often they can be seen sitting on a branch, cliff ledge, fence post, telephone pole or wire, scanning the ground for hours at a time.

The Cooper's hawk, an accipiter from the forests of North America, "still-hunts," waiting patiently and quietly on hidden perches, even near bird feeders. When a bird, such as a blue jay, happens near, the Cooper's will dash out of cover quickly, extend its long legs, and snatch the bird before it can react.

Perch-hunting is one method used by the northern goshawk to catch birds and small mammals. This aggressive accipiter moves from perch to perch along the edge of a clearing in the forest, dropping quickly almost straight to the ground, then pulling up suddenly and landing quietly in an adjacent tree, having barely flapped a wing. This limits the amount of time that the hawk is visible to its prey and also gives the hawk many different vantage points to hunt from.

PENGUIN BREEDING COLONIES PROVIDE GOOD HUNTING FOR STRIATED CARACARAS ON THE FALKLAND ISLANDS.

On the ground. Some species actually forage, or look for food, by walking around on the ground. Crested caracaras are known for this, turning over branches and cow dung looking for insects, reptiles, and amphibians. The striated caracara wanders among penguin colonies on the southern tip of South America and nearby islands, feeding on eggs and chicks.

Kites from warmer climates can often be seen feeding on the ground at garbage dumps. The savanna hawk from South America will gather in groups at grass fires, walking along the edge of the flames, picking up fleeing small mammals, reptiles, and insects.

6 The Life Cycle

Although hawks spend a lot of time hunting, a good portion of a year in the life of a hawk is taken up with reproduction. The whole cycle—from establishing territory, courtship, nest building, and mating, to raising the young and fledging—may take several months. Females take care of the brooding, or nest-sitting, and males hunt and provide food for the young and the female.

When it comes to reproduction, hawks and falcons are very different. Falcons breed earlier (at one year old) than hawks (at about two to three years old) and have larger clutches, and more eggs per laying, but they need these advantages because they aren't as long-lived as hawks. Merlins, a species of falcon, may live seven or eight years, while a red-tailed hawk may live twenty-four or twenty-five years. So a merlin may only have six or seven chances to breed while a red-tailed hawk may have more than twenty.

LARGE BROODS LIKE THIS SPARROWHAWK'S MEAN THAT THE PARENTS SPEND MUCH OF THEIR TIME FINDING FOOD FOR THE CHICKS.

Hawks and falcons normally mate once a year, during either the summer or dry season, depending upon their range. Breeding is usually timed to coincide with the hatching or birth of a particular raptor's preferred prey species. This means that there will be plenty of food for the parent birds to catch for their young. Falcons breed early in the season because they need to be ready when young songbirds are out and about. All of these songbirds hatch in a relatively short span of time in spring. Hawks and other raptors that have a more varied diet lay their eggs later because there is a more gradual increase in the number of young prey throughout the season. If there is enough food available for a long enough time, some species of hawk, like the black-shouldered kite and the American kestrel, will have more than one clutch. And if the eggs do not hatch or are eaten by a predator, some hawks will lay a second clutch to replace them.

Courtship and Mating

The breeding cycle begins with either newly mature male hawks choosing a breeding territory or with mating pairs occupying their previous year's site. Males return to the breeding grounds earlier than females, to reestablish the pair's territory. The new males will have to attract females to their chosen territory. They take care to choose a location that is safe and has good hunting nearby. In some species the male will then advertise his presence by calling loudly from perches and doing aerial acrobatics. This helps to show off the male's fitness and strength, thereby attracting females. Once the hawks pair up, they often stay together for life.

After they have established a breeding territory or reoccupied an old one, the mating pair begins the process of courtship. Raptors are known for their elaborate courtship displays. Many species do "sky dances" in which one or both birds soar high above the ground, doing swoops, dives, and undulations. Harriers sometimes even do loop-the-loops. This dancing is usually accompanied by calling.

The courting pairs may sometimes engage in mock attacks. The male will dive at the female, who then swings upside down and presents her talons to him. The pair may touch talons briefly before the male veers off and the female rights herself. Some falcons even lock talons and tumble in the sky. This may be practice in some species for passing food, which occurs later in the breeding season. A male carrying a catch back to the nest calls loudly to bring the female out. As she flies up to meet him, she flips, and the male drops the food into her waiting talons. Then she carries the food back to the chicks.

The male feeds the female during the courtship and mating periods. This allows her to build up the necessary energy reserves to grow the eggs and to keep them warm once she lays them.

When mating occurs, the male mounts the female and their cloacas meet, passing sperm from the male to the female. This may happen hundreds of times leading up to egg-laying, as with the northern goshawk.

Nest Building

Depending upon the species and the habitat, raptors build a variety of nests. In general, large raptors build large, strong nests that they reuse each year, while smaller species build smaller, flimsier nests that have to be rebuilt every breeding season. Both the male and female work to construct the nest, but the female usually takes the lead. Often a mating pair will build more than one nest in their territory in case something happens to the nest they start using.

MATING SYSTEMS

roviding for enough young birds to keep the species going requires a lot of work for hawk parents. That's why most species are monogamous. Two birds that mate exclusively with each other is a better guarantee of successful reproduction and the rearing of young. One parent (usually the female) broods—or sits on the eggs and young chicks, keeping them warm—while the other (usually the male) hunts. Mating pairs of most migratory species, like the Australian kestrel, spend the winter apart, but some species, like brown falcons and lesser kestrels, stay together in pairs all year.

THESE HARRIS'S HAWK CHICKS WILL BENEFIT FROM HAVING THREE ADULT BIRDS TO CARE FOR THEM.

In some cases, even two birds aren't enough to raise a brood. Two other breeding systems are rare, but they do occur in hawks and falcons. Harriers are the only group in which polygyny occurs commonly. One male occupies a large territory and mates with several females, usually three. This system makes sense given the ecology of these raptors' habitats and prey. Harriers breed in patchy landscapes, where there are very rich pockets of habitat spread out over a large region. The areas between patches are sparsely vegetated and contain little prey. Within the patches, there are good nest sites and enough prey for one male to provide for many females and their young.

Galápagos hawks practice polyandry, in which one female mates with two or more males. This system occurs where there is limited food available, so it takes two or more males to provide enough food to raise the young.

Harris's hawks practice a very similar breeding system called cooperative breeding, which involves one or more males. But in this case only the dominant male mates with the female. Usually, a young hawk from a previous nesting hangs around the nest, helping to raise the new clutch. This type of breeding increases the success rate of the hatchlings and allows the hawks to mate only every other year.

Most common among hawks, kites, accipiters, caracaras, and some falcons are stick nests built in trees. In fact, around 85 percent of all raptor species make their nests this way. At the beginning of the breeding season, the previous year's nest is added to or fixed if need be. Then, just before egg-laying, a fresh layer of green growth is laid in the nest. This may help to keep the nest clean, and some raptors may even choose species of plants that prevent bacteria or insects from infesting the nest.

Most species of falcon are cliff-nesters. A ledge with an overhang on a cliff face is a secure spot with good views of the surrounding territory. Falcons scrape out a shallow depression in the floor of the ledge that helps to keep the eggs in place. Some species have even been known to nest on flat rooftops in urban areas.

SOME HAWK AND FALCON SPECIES HAVE ADAPTED TO CITY LIFE, FEEDING ON THE LARGE NUMBERS OF PIGEONS, STARLINGS, AND OTHER BIRDS THAT THRIVE THERE.

Many kestrels, forest-falcons, and falconets are cavity nesters, meaning they nest in holes in trees made by woodpeckers or other birds. They also may nest in holes in buildings, or they may use the old nests of raptors, crows, or other birds.

Since their hunting territory is in very open places with few perches or predators, harriers nest on the ground. This is the only group of raptors known to do this exclusively, although some species, like the osprey, may occasionally build ground nests.

Laying and Hatching

Once the nest is built and successful mating accomplished, the female lays the eggs. Smaller species, like falcons, kestrels, and sparrowhawks, may lay up to six eggs, while larger birds, such as true hawks, lay three eggs at most. Eggs are laid between two and three days apart. In almost all species, except some kites, the female broods, or incubates, the eggs. As she gains weight during the courtship period, she develops a brood patch, or a section of extra-warm bare skin on her underside that comes in contact with the eggs and helps to keep them at the right temperature. She turns them over with her beak occasionally so they'll heat evenly and the fluid inside the eggs won't stick to the shell. The incubation period takes about a month—less time for smaller species, more time for larger species.

When the young are ready to emerge from the egg, they start pecking at the shell from the inside with their egg tooth, which will fall off as they grow. Hatching may take one to two days. Once they are free from the shell, these chicks are unable to stand and are mostly blind and helpless. Within about an hour, some species start to move around and accept the small pieces of food that their mother tears from kills. Although they are born with a thin coat of down, they cannot keep themselves

Mating pairs of osprey use a variety of materials from their habitats to build their nests, including driftwood, seaweed, grasses, and even bones.

Because of deforestation, many New Zealand bush falcons now nest in grasslands.

warm and need to be brooded by the mother for up to two weeks, until they grow another, fuller layer of down.

Raising the Young

The chicks grow quickly once they hatch. The beak and talons, the most important tools of a hunting bird, are very large at birth and grow rapidly. They will be nearly full-size when the chick is only half-grown.

Of all the feathers on the growing chick, the flight feathers grow the fastest because they will need to be used as soon as the bird is ready to leave the nest. As the second layer of downy feathers grows, the flight feathers emerge beneath them,

WHILE THIS CRESTED CARACARA CHICK GROWS, ITS PARENTS WILL PROVIDE IT WITH FOOD AND WATER UNTIL IT HAS A FULL FEATHER COAT AND CAN HUNT FOR ITSELF.

growing from the same rachis. The downy tips will break off when the feathers have fully emerged.

As the chicks get bigger and grow a full feather coat they do not need to be brooded any longer. The female parent can then join the male in the hunt. This is fortunate because as the chicks grow, they get more insistent for their food, calling loudly as the parents approach with their kills. Soon this fledging period will be over. In most species this period lasts about as long as the incubation period, around a month. For some larger species it can be much longer, almost twice the incubation period.

A YOUNG OSPREY STRETCHES ITS WINGS SO THAT IT WILL BE READY FOR THE DAY WHEN IT TAKES ITS FIRST FLIGHT.

Leaving the Nest

The young birds will practice flying for a few days before they leave the nest entirely. The parents still bring them food until they get the feel of using their wings. Once they are able to fly more easily, some species still hang around with their parents for a few weeks, hunting with them. Some species, like Harris's hawks, don't disperse that quickly, but stay with the parents for a year or more, helping to raise next year's clutch. Young hawks and falcons know instinctively how to hunt and do not need to be taught. Some falcon parents may bring a live bird back to the nesting area, release it, and let the young catch it, perhaps as a way of practicing.

Most species aren't ready to breed until they are between one and three years old. The young birds may be physically ready but may not be able to secure a territory of their own until a mature bird dies or the young birds are big and confident enough to muscle an adult out of his territory.

7

Hawks, Threatened and Saved

Although there are many species and large numbers of hawks and falcons in the world, they face many dangers. Natural causes of death—such as disease, wounds, and starvation—make mortality high among birds of prey. On average, more than 50 percent of all juvenile raptors die in their first year out of the nest. This figure is even higher in some species—70 percent of young northern sparrowhawks die before they reach breeding age.

These natural dangers make surviving difficult enough for both young and adult hawks and falcons. But when raptors have to compete with humans, many birds wind up losing, with some becoming endangered or even extinct.

Threats

In their religious worship and storytelling, many cultures and peoples have long recognized the important role that winged

A BIOLOGIST IS ADDING EGGS TO THIS PEREGRINE FALCON'S CLIFF NEST SO THE PARENTS WILL INCUBATE THEM AND RAISE THE CHICKS.

predators play in the cycle of life on Earth. But when raptors began to get in the way of mankind's progress, conflicts arose. Ever since the first forests were cut down and the first grasslands plowed under for crops, habitat for raptors has been shrinking. Once livestock and small-game hunting became important parts of our lifestyle, hawks began falling to the trap and the gun. Developments in agricultural practices after World War II—in the form of pesticides, herbicides, and fungicides—brought many species to the edge of extinction.

Habitat Destruction. The habitat needs of hawks and falcons are almost as varied as the number of their species. Most species require a plentiful food source, which in turn relies on large and varied habitats. Once the amount of land suitable for habitats is reduced through cutting trees for building or other materials or converting open space for agricultural purposes, the habitat shrinks and is degraded for the rodents, songbirds, reptiles, amphibians, insects, and other life forms that raptors depend upon.

Birds of prey, like other predators, are at the top of a complex food chain. The species they eat in turn eat other species of plants or animals, which may in turn eat other species, and so on. If their food source or some other component is removed, the whole food chain is disrupted. When grasslands that field mice or voles rely on for certain insects and seeds are plowed under, many rodents may die out or move away. It also affects butterflies that feed on wildflower nectar, birds that eat wild grass seeds, and ultimately the hawks and falcons that feed on many of these species. When monoculture, such as a single large crop of vegetables or a plantation of the same kind of trees, replaces a meadow or a forest that has an untold variety of life forms, it reduces the complexity of the ecosystem, making it unlivable for many species.

And it is not only the amount of habitat that is important for a predator like a hawk; the composition of that habitat is important, too. If the forest that a northern goshawk lives in is chopped up into small, one-acre plots, the forest will no longer be usable for this accipiter. Many songbirds and small mammals that the goshawk relies on for its food cannot live in such small forest patches, so the goshawk will need to find new territory or die.

Forests are constantly being cut down for human use. To avoid harming other species, government and industry must keep in mind the needs of these species when making use of an area's natural resources. In the United States and other developed countries, regulations exist whose purpose is to govern these practices. This helps stem habitat loss for some species, but great losses have already occurred. Much of the forestland in the world has already been cut more than once for use as building materials and paper.

There are many conservation organizations working to protect lands and waters in developed countries. In many poorer countries the need to make money often far outstrips the desire to protect habitats and species diversity. Helping improve the economies of these countries might enable their governments to begin focusing on their rich biodiversity.

Hunting. Knowing how special birds of prey are, it may be difficult to understand why some people hate and persecute these creatures and treat them disrespectfully.

Ranchers in many countries often consider raptors a threat to their livelihood. When they see a hawk feeding on the carcass of one of their lambs or calves, they naturally assume the bird has killed it. This is sometimes the case, but raptors will scavenge dead animals, and they most often prey on the young or sick because they are easier to catch than full-grown, healthy adults. It is unusual for livestock to be killed by raptors.

Since falconry became outdated by the invention of the gun, humans have increasingly viewed raptors as competitors for the very same game—for example, pheasants and rabbits—that they once used these birds to hunt. This distrust of raptors has caused people to kill huge numbers of them over the last century and a half. Millions of raptors were killed by small-game hunters between 1950 and 1970 in Europe alone.

The minor impact that hawks, falcons, and other birds of prey had on the populations of game animals certainly did not justify this wholesale slaughter. In fact, wildlife population biologists have shown us that raptor populations are controlled by prey populations rather than the other way around. If the prey numbers drop, the raptor numbers drop, but predators rarely overhunt their food source.

Despite legislation passed in many countries to protect these and other migratory birds, in some parts of the world birds of prey are still shot down out of the sky. Tens of thousands of the birds are killed by hunters every year in southern Europe alone as they cross the Mediterranean on their migration route.

Raptors are also killed indirectly by guns. Lead bullets in waterfowl downed by hunters but never retrieved are often consumed by raptors when they find and eat these easy meals. The lead shot slowly poisons them, and many eventually die. A program in the United States to phase out lead shot has helped considerably, however.

Pesticides. It wasn't until twenty years after pesticides first began to be commonly used that their danger to both wildlife and humans became known. Rachel Carson's 1962 book, *Silent Spring*, was the world's wake-up call. Organochlorine pesticides such as DDT were linked to worldwide population declines in wildlife, especially predators such as hawks, falcons, and eagles. These chemicals easily leached into soils and waterways and drifted on air currents, even to remote locations. Scientists actually couldn't find any birds that didn't have pesticides in their systems.

DDT is very stable in the environment, persisting for many years. As plants and insects become contaminated, the toxin builds in fatty tissues of animals that eat them. This concentration becomes even greater in raptors' bodies when they prey on these animals. Accipiters, falcons, and other bird-eating raptors were most affected because the long food chain gave the toxins more chance to become concentrated. DDT didn't kill the raptors outright but caused their eggshells to become so thin they were crushed by the weight of the mother incubating them. This caused widespread and continual nesting failure in many species. The populations of ospreys, peregrine falcons, and bald eagles were particularly badly hurt.

Other organochlorine pesticides such as dieldrin and aldrin are more directly lethal, killing birds outright. Many of these and other harmful pesticides were outlawed in some countries, such as the United States. But their widespread use in poorer countries with few environmental regulations still causes many deaths and major problems in raptor productivity since most of the world's bird populations migrate and winter in these Southern Hemisphere countries.

Protection

Despite all the human-caused threats to birds of prey, people have done a lot to prevent or reverse the causes of species decline over the last thirty years. From legislation to captive-breeding programs, humankind is seeking ways to bring these birds back from the edge of extinction.

Laws. Once the world became aware of what pesticides were doing to the environment, humans, and wildlife, governments and other organizations began to take action. The International Union for Conservation of Nature and Natural Resources (IUCN), now called IUCN—The World Conservation Union, and the International Council for Bird Preservation (ICBP) published the first Red Data Book in 1966. This list of all endangered, vulnerable, and rare birds worldwide helped make people aware of how many species were in trouble and of the threats they faced. The list is still published and updated every few years.

FEEDING THIS CAPTIVE-BRED
PEREGRINE FALCON CHICK USING
A HAND PUPPET PAINTED TO
LOOK LIKE AN ADULT PEREGRINE
PREVENTS THE CHICK FROM
BONDING WITH HUMANS.

Also in 1966 the United States passed the Endangered
Species Preservation Act, followed in 1972 by the first U.S. list of
endangered species. After changes were made to the act to
include all plant and animal groups—threatened as well as
endangered species and ecosystems —and language was added
to prevent endangered species from being imported or export-
ed, the Endangered Species Act (ESA) was adopted in 1973. By
1972, other federal and state legislation had been adopted that
protected all raptor species from persecution.

This awareness of environmental dangers led to other
protection for wildlife as well. The Convention on International

THIS IMMATURE HAWK IS BEING BANDED—HAVING A SMALL METAL BAND WITH
IDENTIFYING NUMBERS ATTACHED TO ITS FOOT. IF THIS BIRD IS RECAPTURED,
RESEARCHERS WILL BE ABLE TO TELL HOW FAR THE BIRD HAS FLOWN AND PERHAPS
EVEN HOW OLD IT IS.

Trade in Endangered Species of Wild Flora and Fauna (CITES)
was held in 1973, and a treaty was signed by 120 countries, providing international protection for endangered species.

Raptor populations were also helped by the banning of the
sale and use of DDT in Britain and Europe in 1970, in Canada in
1971, and in the United States in 1972. Raptor populations hit
their lowest point in that year, but they have been on a steady
increase since.

Education. Over the last three decades many groups have
formed that are dedicated solely to raptor species recovery.
Raptor rehabilitation centers provide veterinarian services to
injured wild raptors. The main goal of these centers is to heal
the birds so they can be released back into the wild. But sometimes the injuries are too serious and a bird would not be able
to survive if it were released. Some of these unreleasable birds

are cared for and kept on display at the centers so visitors can see and learn about them. This exposure, in addition to educational programs that the centers offer, helps to open the public's eyes to the world of raptors and enables people to appreciate these amazing creatures face-to-face.

Management. Conserving habitat for birds of prey is the best way to help them. One outstanding example is Idaho's Snake River Birds of Prey Area, a 610,000-acre (247,000-hectare) property that is home to more than 700 pairs of 15 different species of raptors. Managed by the United States Bureau of Land Management (BLM), its primary mission is "the preservation of this impressive raptor community and the habitat it requires."

While there may be suitable habitat available for some hawks and falcons, some populations are so low that the individuals can't reproduce quickly enough to keep the species from dying out. So some rehabilitation centers and government and private organizations are working to correct that. One technique they use is to raise endangered and threatened species of raptors in captivity through a program of captive breeding. The aim is to return these birds to their natural habitats so they can repopulate areas where they had been wiped out. The Peregrine Fund, a private conservation group, was the first organization to successfully raise many raptors of different species for reintroduction. In 1973 they released the first captive-bred peregrine falcon into the wild after the species was wiped out in the eastern United States. By 1990 the group had released more than 3,300 falcons into their native habitats.

In some cases adult wild birds are healthy but cannot have successful clutches because of eggshell thinning from pesticide poisoning or other reasons. To bolster the population, normal eggs from a healthy mating pair can be put into the unsuccessful pair's nest to be raised. The healthy pair will lay another batch

of eggs that they will raise on their own. With enough nests, this
technique, called double-clutching, can raise the numbers of a
species significantly over several years. This was one of the techniques used to bring back the peregrine falcon.

Artificial nesting platforms or nest boxes are one way that
wildlife managers and conservationists help to encourage nesting.
Many species, like the osprey, respond well to these structures.
Preferring to nest near water, these birds often find that they
have no choice but to nest on the ground because there are not
enough trees. This increases the chance that their eggs will
fall victim to predators, like coyotes or red foxes. Government

agencies have erected many nesting platforms—flat boards or large tires on poles—that the ospreys use readily. This method has helped osprey populations increase to record high numbers.

Endangered Hawks

Recent years have seen some amazing successes in recovery of endangered and threatened birds of prey. In 1999 the United States Fish and Wildlife Service (USFWS) removed the American peregrine falcon from the endangered species list and proposed taking the bald eagle off the list as well.

The IUCN's current Red Data Book (2000) lists seventy-three species of diurnal raptors as endangered, rare, or vulnerable.

THIS CAPTIVE-BRED FALCON CHICK IS BEING WEIGHED TO MAKE SURE IT IS GAINING ENOUGH WEIGHT AND AT THE CORRECT RATE. THE CHICK NEEDS TO GROW UP STRONG AND HEALTHY SO IT CAN BE RELEASED TO THE WILD.

Some of the more charismatic and well-known species, such as the bald eagle and the peregrine falcon, have received a lot of attention and funding for their recovery. But many lesser-known species, especially those in poor, densely populated countries, are still in serious trouble, with little protection or conservation efforts afforded them.

Guadalupe caracara (*Caracara lutosus*)

Given the number of raptors currently in danger of extinction worldwide, it is surprising that the Guadalupe caracara is the only raptor known to have become extinct in the last 400 years. Closely related to the crested caracara, this bird lived only on Isla Guadalupe, in Mexico. It was probably killed off by settlers on the island who may have thought it was attacking their livestock. The last known bird was recorded in 1900.

Réunion harrier (*Circus maillardi*)

Formerly lumped as one species with the Madagascar harrier, the Réunion harrier's new status as a distinct species means that this bird is even more endangered than its relative. This harrier is hunted and killed on its tiny island home of Réunion, off the coast of Madagascar, because locals believe it kills their chickens. Habitat destruction and road-building are also affecting the 340 or so birds left on the island. But despite these threats, numbers are thought to be increasing due to protection efforts in effect since 1974.

Cuban kite (*Chondrohierax wilsonii, subspecies of hook-billed kite, C. uncinatus*)

Cuba's rarest raptor, the Cuban kite, has not been so lucky. The very small population—at most 250 birds—is shrinking due to logging, agricultural conversion of lands, the decline of its food source, and because the Cuban kite is mistakenly persecuted and hunted as a chicken-killer. This large, snail-eating kite with a big yellow bill is now confined to a small area in the east of the country and is thought to be on the verge of extinction.

Mauritius kestrel (*Falco punctatus*)

Another island resident off the coast of Madagascar, the Mauritius kestrel has increased its numbers due to intensive conservation efforts. Limited to the tiny island of Mauritius, this species was the victim of introduced predators—rats, feral (once domestic, now wild) cats, and mongooses—and pesticide poisoning. Efforts including captive breeding, nest box provision, nest guarding, and treatment of sick birds have brought the population up from only four birds in 1974 to nearly 400 in 1999.

Galápagos hawk (*Buteo galapagoensis*)

Formerly native to all fourteen Galápagos Islands, the Galápagos hawk is now restricted to nine. While the population is considered stable and the islands are a national park, this endemic hawk is still vulnerable to extinction. Human persecution continues today despite the hawk being protected by Ecuadorean law since 1959. Competition with other predators for food also keeps their numbers low.

The Future for Hawks

With their history stretching back hundreds of millions of years, hawks and falcons have adapted to and endured a startlingly large number and wide variety of dangers, including meteors, climate change, continental drift, and competition with dinosaurs, the fiercest predators that ever lived. Not only are they masters of the air, hawks and falcons are also able to take advantage of the

other realms of the world—land and water. Their ability to exploit all the different food sources of these three realms is what makes this group of birds so diverse and successful.

But despite their long history and tenacity, hawks may in fact go the way of their close relatives, the dinosaurs, if humankind's current overexploitation of the world's natural resources continues in reckless disregard for other life forms. If these birds become casualties of our progress, it will not be long before all humans realize how necessary these and all other creatures are to the healthy functioning of our ecosystems and the biosphere as a whole. It is difficult and frightening to imagine, but a time might come when the wonder and beauty of a wall of Eleonora's falcons intercepting songbirds above the Mediterranean Sea, an osprey defying the ocean realm for its meals, or the hair-raising cry of a red-tailed hawk circling in the sky will no longer be around to inspire us.

AS LONG AS HUMANS RESPECT THEM, THE FUTURE OF THESE GALÁPAGOS HAWKS AND OF ALL RAPTORS MAY NOT BE AS SHAKY AS A SKINNY PERCH IN A STRONG WIND.

Glossary

austringer—a person who hunts with hawks or eagles

barb—one of the many small, thin parts that make up the vane of the feather

barbule—tiny hooklike parts that hold the barbs together; they allow a bird to "zip" its feathers closed so they are smooth, aerodynamic, and water-repellent

biodiversity—the grouping of species in an ecosystem, including soil organisms, fungus, wildflowers, trees, insects, reptiles, amphibians, birds, and mammals

breed—to give birth or hatch

breeding cycle—the entire process of reproduction in hawks and falcons, including courtship, mating, nest building, hatching, incubation, fledging, and post-fledging

brood—to sit on and hatch eggs; to keep young hawks warm by sitting on or next to them

brood patch— a patch of bare flesh with extra blood vessels on the underside of female birds that is used to keep eggs and chicks warm

captive breeding—the practice of raising young hawks or other animals in captivity, such as in a zoo or other location that is not the animal's natural habitat

carnivore—an organism, usually an animal, that eats meat

carrion—the meat of dead and decaying animals

cere—the area of bare skin between a hawk's eyes and its beak; it helps to keep the area around the eyes and mouth clean

cloaca—the opening beneath the tail on a bird's body, inside which are the intestinal, genital, and urinary tracts

cooperative breeding—the practice of sharing the duties of raising young among a family group, as in Harris's hawks

crop—a pouch in a bird's throat where food is stored before its slow release into the stomach

dihedral—a V-shaped angle; some soaring raptors hold their wings this way, such as harriers and turkey vultures

dispersal—the time when a young bird leaves its parents' care and seeks out its own territory

double-clutching—inducing a bird to lay a second set, or clutch, of eggs by removing the first set from the nest; this method is used to increase numbers of a threatened or endangered population, such as the peregrine falcon

egg tooth—the small, bony knob on a newborn chick's bill used to break open the eggshell at hatching

endangered—a designation indicating that a bird, plant, or other organism is in danger of extinction

endemic—native to and existing only in a particular location, such as an island or a country

extinction—the dying out of a species, such as the Guadalupe caracara or the passenger pigeon

falconer—a person who hunts with falcons

fledging period—the early time of a bird's life, from hatching to dispersal

gizzard—a muscular pouch behind a bird's stomach that helps break down food for digestion

habitat—the type of environment where an animal lives; for example, a grassland or a desert

hatchling—a newly hatched bird; a chick

jesses—leather strips tied to a raptor's feet that are used to restrain the bird and leash it to the falconer's glove

migrate—to move from one home to another on a regular, usually seasonal, basis to take advantage of food sources; some hawks and falcons migrate long distances, from Canada to South America, for example

monogamy—the practice of a male and female mating exclusively for life

morphology—the form and structure of a hawk or other creature

pesticide—a chemical used to protect crops from insects and disease

pirating—stealing food from another bird, as when a bald eagle steals food from an osprey

plumage—a bird's coat of feathers

predator—an animal that preys on other animals; for example, a hawk or a wolf

prey—animals that a predator hunts and eats

primary feathers—the leading flight feathers on the hand of the wing of a bird; these are used for flapping and adjusting to turbulence

reproduction—the process of creating new organisms of the same kind

savanna—a flat grassland of tropical or subtropical regions

secondary feathers—the flight feathers on the wing of a bird closest to the body and next to the primary feathers; these help to hold the air and keep the bird aloft

stoop—a headfirst dive used by some species of falcon to kill and/or knock prey out of the sky or to attack them on the ground or in the water

talons—sharp, clawlike nails on the tips of the toes of raptors used for catching and killing prey

tarsus—on a bird, the part of the leg below the knee; the plural of "tarsus" is tarsi

threatened—a designation indicating that a bird, plant, or other organism could become endangered if measures aren't undertaken to aid its recovery

updrafts—winds that are deflected upward by mountains or other formations and used by raptors to aid migratory flight

Species Checklist

This is a list of all the hawks and falcons discussed in this book. For a more thorough list of the 221 species of hawks and falcons in 46 genera in the world, please refer to Ferguson-Lees' Raptors of the World or Dr. Ian Newton's Birds of Prey. New species are being discovered or split from other species as DNA analysis becomes more widely used in ornithology.

Common Name	Scientific Species Name

Order Falconiformes

Family Accipitridae

Osprey

Osprey	*Pandion haliaetus*

Kites, Bazas, and Honey-buzzards

Western honey-buzzard	*Pernis apivorus*
Eastern honey-buzzard	*Pernis ptilorhyncus*
Black-shouldered kite	*Elanus caeruleus*
Letter-winged kite	*Elanus scriptus*
Snail kite	*Rostrhamus sociabilis*
Brahminy kite	*Haliastur Indus*
Hook-billed kite	*Chondrohierax uncinatus*
Cuban kite	*Chondrohierax wilsonii*

Harriers and harrier-hawks

Northern harrier	*Circus hudsonius*
African marsh harrier	*Circus ranivorus*
Malagasy marsh harrier	*Circus maillardi*
Réunion harrier	*Circus maillardi*

True Accipiters

Tiny hawk	*Accipiter superciliosus*
Northern sparrowhawk	*Accipiter nisus*
Sharp-shinned hawk	*Accipiter striatus*
Cooper's hawk	*Accipiter cooperii*
Northern goshawk	*Accipiter gentilis*

True Hawks and Buzzards

Harris's (or Bay-winged) hawk	*Parabuteo unicinctus*
Swainson's hawk	*Buteo swainsoni*
Galapagos hawk	*Buteo galapagoensis*
Red-tailed hawk	*Buteo jamaicensis*
Rough-legged hawk	*Buteo lagopus*
Jackal buzzard	*Buteo rufofuscus*
Gray hawk	*Buteo nitidus*
Savannah hawk	*Buteogallus meridionalis*

Family Falconidae

Caracaras

Striated (Forster's) caracara	*Phalcoboenus australis*
Crested caracara	*Caracara plancus*
Guadalupe caracara	*Caracara lutosus*

Laughing falcons and Forest-falcons

Barred forest-falcon	*Micrastur ruficollis*

Pygmy-falcons and Old World falconets

African pygmy-falcon	*Polihierax semitorquatus*
White-rumped pygmy-falcon	*Polihierax insignis*
Bornean falconet	*Microhierax latifrons*
Philippine falconet	*Microhierax erythrogenys*

Falcons

American kestrel	*Falco sparverius*
Common kestrel	*Falco tinnunculus*
Mauritius kestrel	*Falco punctatus*
Australian kestrel	*Falco cenchroides*
Red-headed falcon	*Falco chicquera*
Eastern red-footed falcon	*Falco amurensis*
Eleonora's falcon	*Falco eleonorae*
Sooty falcon	*Falco concolor*
Merlin	*Falco columbarius*
Prairie falcon	*Falco mexicanus*
Lanner falcon	*Falco biarmicus*
Peregrine falcon	*Falco peregrinus*

Further Research

Books

Dunne, Pete. *The Wind Masters: The Lives of North American Birds of Prey*.
Boston: Houghton Mifflin Company, 1995.
Profiles of North American raptors written from each bird's point
of view.

Pasquier, Roger F. *Watching Birds: An Introduction to Ornithology*. Boston:
Houghton Mifflin Company. 1980.

Sutton, Clay, and Patricia Taylor Sutton. *How to Spot Hawks and Eagles*.
Shelburne, VT: Chapters Publishing, Inc., 1996.
A very informative and readable guide to watching raptors, with
information about migration viewing sites.

Web Sites

http://www.camacdonald.com/birding/Sampler5.htm
Birding site shows photos of raptors of the world and provides links to
information on birding all over the world.

http://www.birdlife.net
BirdLife International's Web site provides a lot of information about
birds, birding, endangered species and ecosystems, and conservation
efforts.

http://www.natureserve.org/
NatureServe is a leading source for information about rare and
endangered species and threatened ecosystems.

http://www.peregrinefund.org/index.html
The Peregrine Fund is an international organization that helps to protect
birds of prey through captive breeding and conservation projects.

http://www.raptor.cvm.umn.edu/
The Raptor Center of the University of Minnesota provides information
on raptors and the center's rehabilitation efforts.

http://theraptortrust.org
The Raptor Trust in Millington, New Jersey, provides information on
raptors, building nest boxes, and the resident raptors at the Trust.

http://www.id.blm.gov/bopnca/index.html
> The Snake River Birds of Prey National Conservation Area Web site offers descriptions and maps of the natural area and a raptor identification guide, among other good information.

http://www.vinsweb.org/raptor=center/index.html
> The Vermont Raptor Center site offers information on raptor rehabilitation and programs.

Bibliography

Allan, David. *Birds of Prey of Southern, Central, and East Africa*. London: New Holland Publishers, Ltd., 1996.

BirdLife International, Species Factsheets, http://www.birdlife.net

Bond, James. *Peterson Field Guides: Birds of the West Indies*. Boston: Houghton Mifflin Company, 1993.

Brown, Leslie, and Dean Amadon. *Eagles, Hawks, and Falcons of the World*. Vols. 1 and 2. New York: McGraw-Hill Book Co., 1968.

Chatterjee, Sankar. *The Rise of Birds*. Baltimore, MD: Johns Hopkins University Press, 1997.

Clark, William S., and Brian K. Wheeler. *Peterson Field Guides: Hawks of North America*. Boston: Houghton Mifflin Company, 2001.

Ferguson-Lees, James, and David A. Christie. *Raptors of the World*. Boston: Houghton Mifflin Company, 2001.

Gill, Frank B. *Ornithology*. New York: W. H. Freeman and Co., 1990.

Grossman, Mary L., and John Hamlet. *Birds of Prey of the World*. New York: Clarkson N. Potter, Inc., 1964.

IUCN Red List of Threatened Species, http://www.redlist.org.

Johnsgard, Paul A. *Hawks, Eagles, and Falcons of North America*. Washington, D.C.: Smithsonian Institution Press, 1990.

Newton, Dr. Ian. *Birds of Prey*. San Francisco: Fog City Press, 2000.

Padian, Kevin, and Luis M. Chiappe. "The Origin of Birds and Their Flight." *Scientific American*, February 1998.

Proctor, Noble S., and Patrick J. Lynch. *Manual of Ornithology*. New Haven: Yale University Press, 1993.

Prum, Richard O., and Alan H. Brush. "Which Came First, the Feather or the Bird?" *Scientific American*, March 2003, pp. 84–93.

United States Fish and Wildlife Service. "A Guide to the Laws and Treaties of the United States for Protecting Migratory Birds." http://migratorybirds.fws.gov/intrnltr/treatlaw.html
Weidensaul, Scott. *The Raptor Almanac*. New York: The Lyons Press, 2000.

Index

Page numbers in **boldface** are charts and illustrations.

About the Author

TOM WARHOL is a writer, photographer, and naturalist. Tom has worked for The Nature Conservancy, managing nature preserves, and he has volunteered for the Vermont Raptor Center, caring for sick and injured hawks, eagles, and owls. Tom's first book in the Animalways series was *Eagles*. He is also the photographer for a forthcoming book on the rivers of eastern North America. Warhol lives in Somerville, Massachusetts.